GIGI Kids' Gratitude Journal

25 days of thanks

GIGI Kids' Gratitude Journal - 25 days of thanks

Published by 5 Sisters Ministry

P.O. BOX 6505, Upper Mt Gravatt, Australia 4122

Visit www.gigistorylibrary.com.au.

ISBN: 978-0-6454319-2-6

Copyright © 2022

Images used under licence from Depositphotos.com

Scripture taken from the Easy-to-Read Version® Copyright © 2006 by Bible League International. Used by permission. All rights reserved.

All rights reserved. No part of this publication may be reproduced, stored, or transmitted in any form without written permission of the publisher–except for brief quotations in printed reviews.

GIGI Kids' Gratitude Journal

25 days of thanks

5 Sisters Ministry
Brisbane, Australia

Hey GIGI kids,

Welcome to your gratitude journal. This book is the special place where you will write and draw things you are thankful for.

God loves it when you have a grateful heart. When you thank Him, you put a big smile on His face! How cool is that!?

Every day for the next 25 days, you can start or end your day with Jesus by writing in this journal.

We hope you enjoy it.

Happy journaling!

Esther and Poppy ♥

PS: Listen to Esther and Poppy tell awesome Christian stories on their podcast called *Car Ride Stories for GIGI Kids.*

THIS JOURNAL BELONGS TO
_____

All about me!

God created me SPECIAL and UNIQUE

My portrait

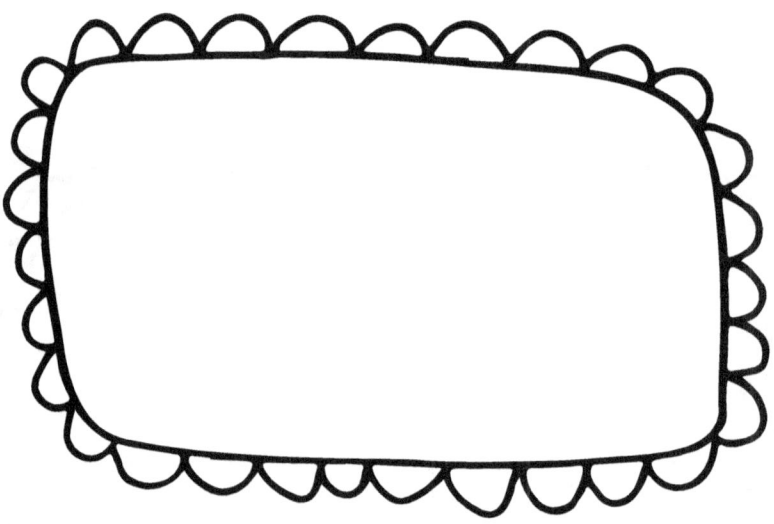

My family

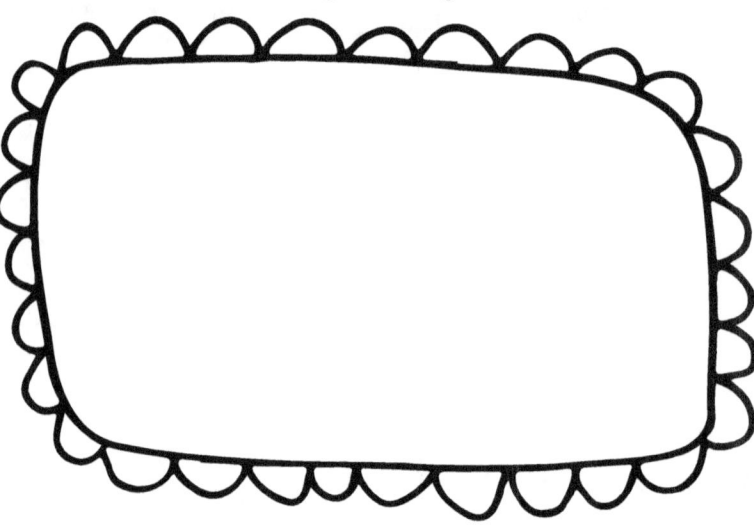

My Favourite things

My favourite bible verse: _____

My favourite bible story: _____

My favourite bible hero: _____

My favourite worship song: _____

My favourite book: _____

My favourite place: _____

My favourite colour: _____

My favourite food: _____

My favourite animal: _____

My favourite sport: _____

Date _____

MY VERSE OF THE DAY

Give thanks to the Lord because he is good....
1 Chronicles 16:34 ERV

A person I am grateful for....

_____
_____
_____
_____
_____
_____

One thing I liked about yesterday....

_____
_____
_____
_____
_____

I am grateful for....

One thing in nature, I am grateful God created.
(Draw it below)

Dear Jesus, thank you for......

_____
_____
_____
_____

Date _____

MY VERSE OF THE DAY

Be kind and loving to each other....
Ephesians 4:32 ERV

A person I am grateful for....

_____
_____
_____
_____
_____
_____
_____

One thing I liked about yesterday....

_____
_____
_____
_____
_____
_____

I am grateful for....

One thing in nature, I am grateful God created.

(Draw it below)

Dear Jesus, thank you for......

_____
_____
_____
_____

Date _____

MY VERSE OF THE DAY

Never stop praying. Be ready for anything by praying and being thankful.
Colossians 4:2 ERV

A person I am grateful for....

_____
_____
_____
_____
_____
_____

One thing I liked about yesterday....

I am grateful for....

One thing in nature, I am grateful God created.
(Draw it below)

Dear Jesus, thank you for......

_____
_____
_____
_____

Date _____

MY VERSE OF THE DAY

We love because God first loved us.
1 John 4:19 ERV

A person I am grateful for....

_____
_____
_____
_____
_____
_____

One thing I liked about yesterday....

_____
_____
_____
_____
_____

I am grateful for....

One thing in nature, I am grateful God created.
(Draw it below)

Dear Jesus, thank you for......

_____
_____
_____
_____

Date _____

MY VERSE OF THE DAY

> I will praise God's name in song.
> I will honor him by giving him thanks.
> Psalm 69:30 ERV

A person I am grateful for....

_____
_____
_____
_____
_____

One thing I liked about yesterday....

_____
_____
_____
_____
_____

I am grateful for....

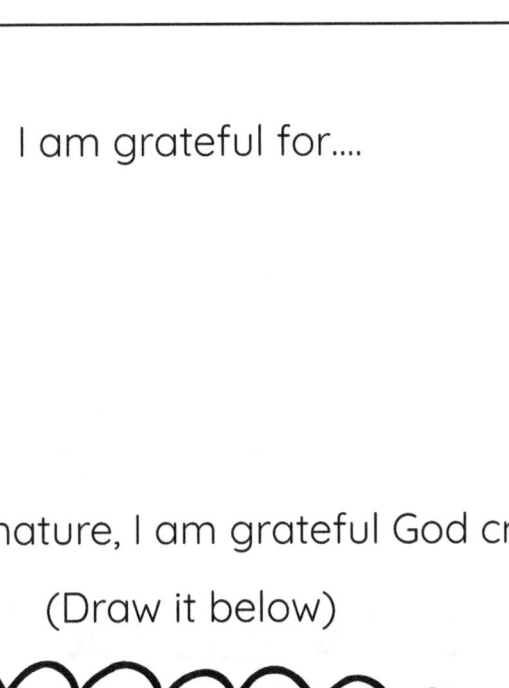

One thing in nature, I am grateful God created.

(Draw it below)

Dear Jesus, thank you for......

_____
_____
_____
_____

Be kind to all creatures big and small

Date _____

MY VERSE OF THE DAY

But Jesus said, "Let the little children come to me. Don't stop them……"
Matthew 19:14 ERV

A person I am grateful for….

_____
_____
_____
_____
_____

One thing I liked about yesterday….

I am grateful for....

One thing in nature, I am grateful God created.

(Draw it below)

Dear Jesus, thank you for......

_____
_____
_____
_____

Date _____

MY VERSE OF THE DAY

.... Ask God for everything you need,
always giving thanks for what you have.
Philippians 4:6 ERV

A person I am grateful for....

_____
_____
_____
_____
_____
_____

One thing I liked about yesterday....

_____
_____
_____
_____
_____

I am grateful for....

One thing in nature, I am grateful God created.

(Draw it below)

Dear Jesus, thank you for......

_____
_____
_____
_____

Date _____

MY VERSE OF THE DAY

You are young, but don't let anyone treat
you as if you are not important.
1 Timothy 4:12 ERV

A person I am grateful for....

_____
_____
_____
_____
_____
_____

One thing I liked about yesterday....

_____
_____
_____
_____
_____

I am grateful for....

One thing in nature, I am grateful God created.

(Draw it below)

Dear Jesus, thank you for......

_____
_____
_____
_____

Date _____

MY VERSE OF THE DAY

The Lord is my shepherd. I will always have everything I need.
Psalms 23:1 ERV

A person I am grateful for....

_____
_____
_____
_____
_____
_____

One thing I liked about yesterday....

_____
_____
_____
_____
_____

I am grateful for....

One thing in nature, I am grateful God created.

(Draw it below)

Dear Jesus, thank you for......

_____
_____
_____
_____

Date _____

MY VERSE OF THE DAY

Yes, God loved the world so much
that he gave his only Son......
John 3:16 ERV

A person I am grateful for....

One thing I liked about yesterday....

I am grateful for....

One thing in nature, I am grateful God created.

(Draw it below)

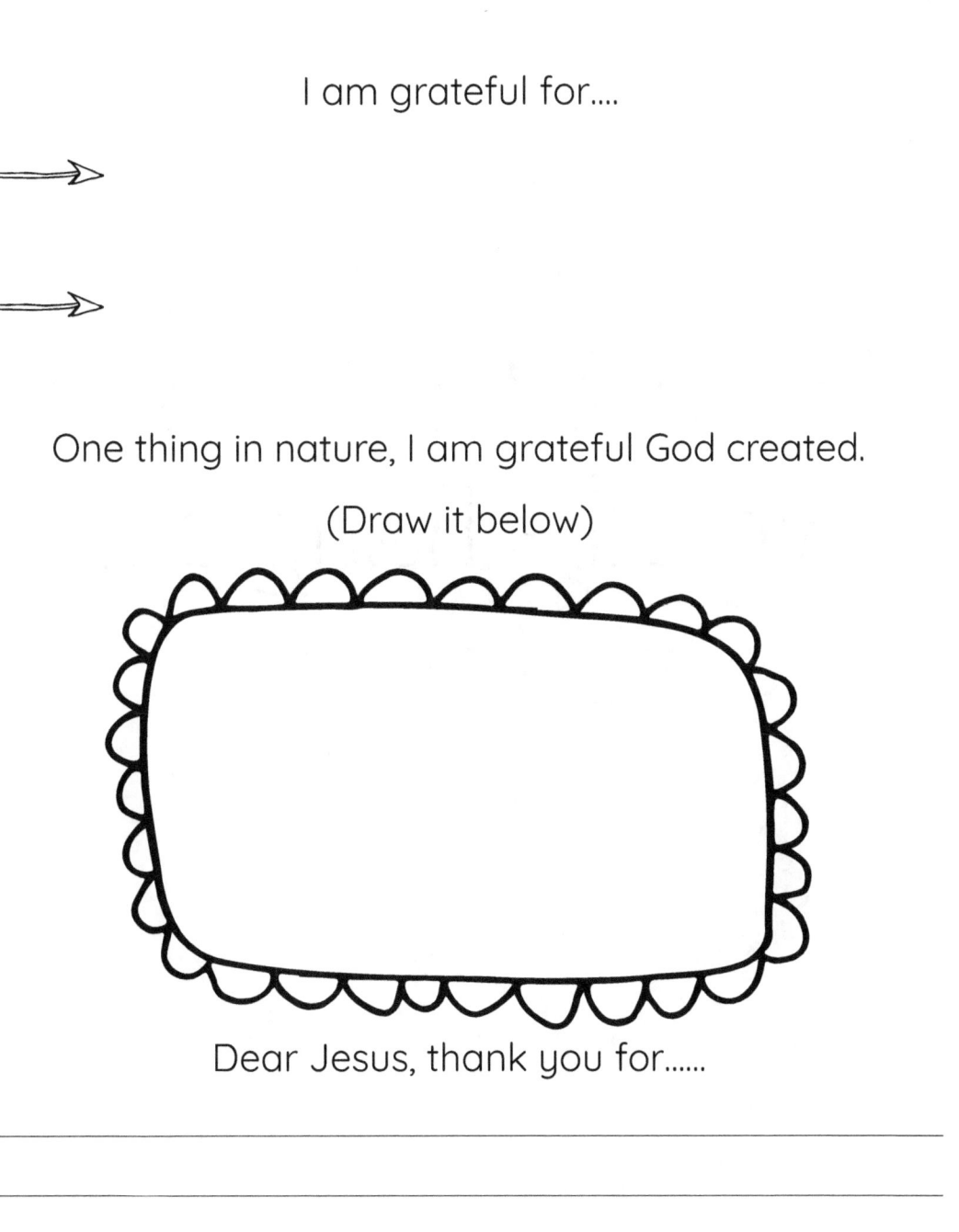

Dear Jesus, thank you for......

_____
_____
_____
_____

Explore the outside world - hang out in nature

Date _____

MY VERSE OF THE DAY

Praise the Lord because he is good.....
Psalms 136:1 ERV

A person I am grateful for....

One thing I liked about yesterday....

I am grateful for....

One thing in nature, I am grateful God created.

(Draw it below)

Dear Jesus, thank you for......

_____
_____
_____
_____

Date _____

MY VERSE OF THE DAY

Do for others what you want them to do for you.
Luke 6:31 ERV

A person I am grateful for....

_____
_____
_____
_____
_____
_____

One thing I liked about yesterday....

_____
_____
_____
_____
_____

I am grateful for....

One thing in nature, I am grateful God created.

(Draw it below)

Dear Jesus, thank you for......

_____
_____
_____
_____

Date _____

MY VERSE OF THE DAY

But we thank God who gives us the victory through our Lord Jesus Christ!
1 Corinthians 15:57 ERV

A person I am grateful for....

_____
_____
_____
_____
_____

One thing I liked about yesterday....

I am grateful for....

One thing in nature, I am grateful God created.

(Draw it below)

Dear Jesus, thank you for......

_____
_____
_____
_____

Date _____

MY VERSE OF THE DAY

Trust the Lord completely.......
Proverbs 3:5 ERV

A person I am grateful for....

_____
_____
_____
_____
_____
_____

One thing I liked about yesterday....

_____
_____
_____
_____
_____

I am grateful for....

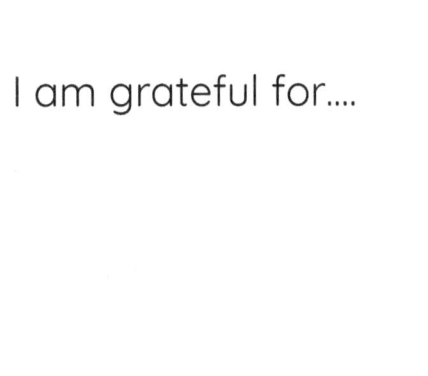

One thing in nature, I am grateful God created.

(Draw it below)

Dear Jesus, thank you for......

_____
_____
_____
_____

Date _____

MY VERSE OF THE DAY

Everything you say and everything you do should be done for Jesus your Lord.......
Colossians 3:17 ERV

A person I am grateful for....

_____
_____
_____
_____
_____
_____

One thing I liked about yesterday....

_____
_____
_____
_____
_____

I am grateful for....

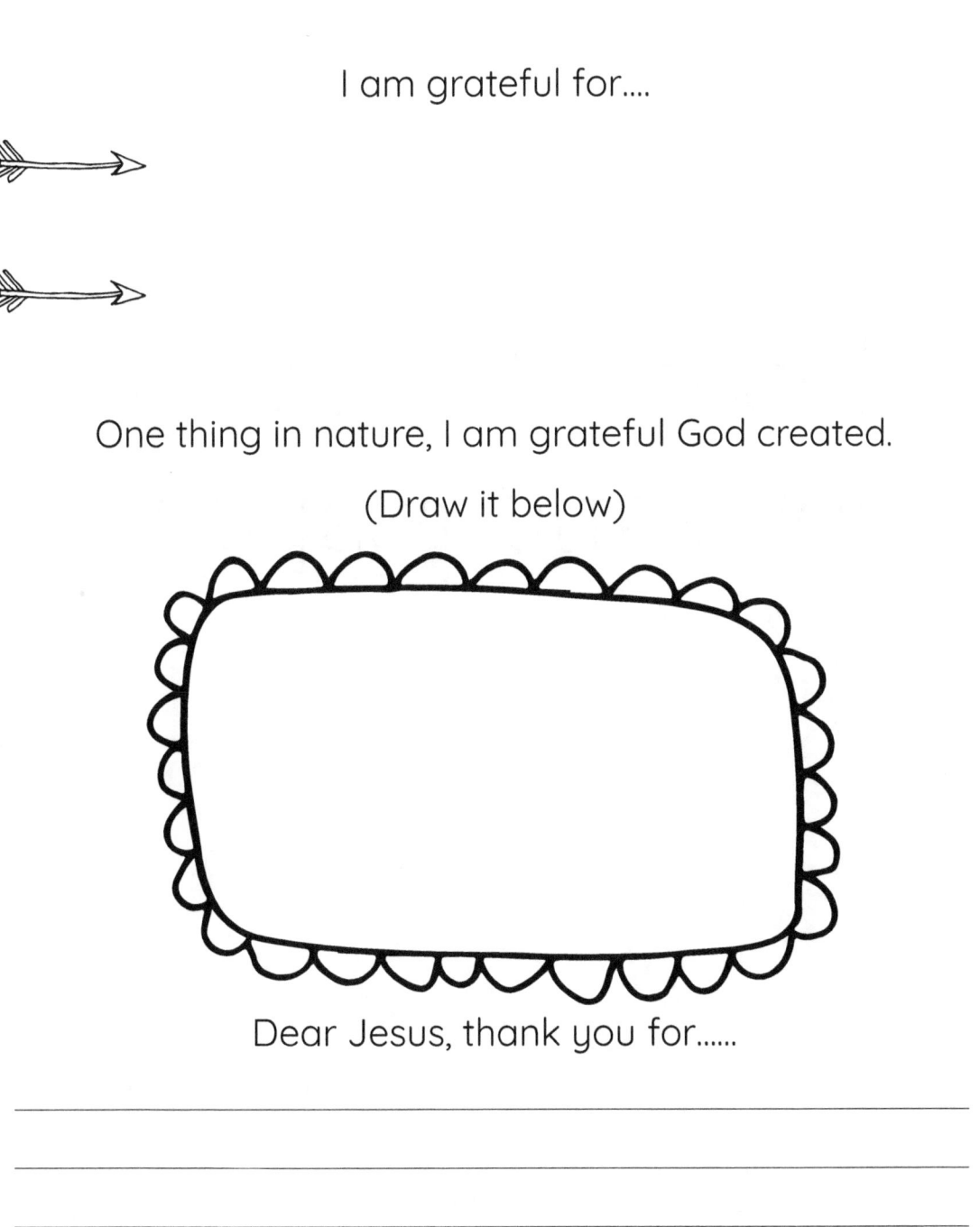

One thing in nature, I am grateful God created.

(Draw it below)

Dear Jesus, thank you for......

_____
_____
_____
_____

Treat others with love and respect

Date _____

MY VERSE OF THE DAY

When I am afraid, I put my trust in you.
Psalms 56:3 ERV

A person I am grateful for....

_____
_____
_____
_____
_____

One thing I liked about yesterday....

_____
_____
_____
_____

I am grateful for....

One thing in nature, I am grateful God created.

(Draw it below)

Dear Jesus, thank you for......

_____
_____
_____
_____

Date _____

MY VERSE OF THE DAY

God is our protection and source of strength.
He is always ready to help us in times of trouble.
Psalm 46:1 ERV

A person I am grateful for....

_____
_____
_____
_____
_____

One thing I liked about yesterday....

_____
_____
_____
_____
_____

I am grateful for....

One thing in nature, I am grateful God created.

(Draw it below)

Dear Jesus, thank you for......

_____
_____
_____
_____

Date _____

MY VERSE OF THE DAY

When you are angry, don't let that anger make you sin, and don't stay angry all day.
Ephesians 4:26 ERV

A person I am grateful for....

_____
_____
_____
_____
_____

One thing I liked about yesterday....

_____
_____
_____
_____
_____

I am grateful for....

One thing in nature, I am grateful God created.

(Draw it below)

Dear Jesus, thank you for......

_____
_____
_____
_____

Date _____

MY VERSE OF THE DAY

Your word is like a lamp that guides my steps,
a light that shows the path I should take.
Psalms 119:105 ERV

A person I am grateful for....

_____
_____
_____
_____
_____

One thing I liked about yesterday....

_____
_____
_____
_____

I am grateful for....

One thing in nature, I am grateful God created.

(Draw it below)

Dear Jesus, thank you for......

_____
_____
_____
_____

Date _____

MY VERSE OF THE DAY

The Lord is with me, so I will not be afraid.
No one on earth can do anything to harm me.
Psalms 118:6 ERV

A person I am grateful for....

_____
_____
_____
_____
_____

One thing I liked about yesterday....

_____
_____
_____
_____
_____

I am grateful for....

One thing in nature, I am grateful God created.

(Draw it below)

Dear Jesus, thank you for......

_____
_____
_____
_____

Be brave and strong in God

Date _____

MY VERSE OF THE DAY

God created the sky and the earth.
Genesis 1:1 ERV

A person I am grateful for....

_____
_____
_____
_____
_____
_____

One thing I liked about yesterday....

_____
_____
_____
_____
_____

I am grateful for....

One thing in nature, I am grateful God created.

(Draw it below)

Dear Jesus, thank you for......

_____
_____
_____
_____

Date _____

MY VERSE OF THE DAY

The heavens tell about the glory of God.
The skies announce what his hands have made.
Psalm 19:1 ERV

A person I am grateful for....

One thing I liked about yesterday....

I am grateful for....

One thing in nature, I am grateful God created.

(Draw it below)

Dear Jesus, thank you for......

_____
_____
_____
_____

Date _____

MY VERSE OF THE DAY

....I give you peace in a different way than the world does. So don't be troubled. Don't be afraid.
John 14:27 ERV

A person I am grateful for....

One thing I liked about yesterday....

I am grateful for....

One thing in nature, I am grateful God created.

(Draw it below)

Dear Jesus, thank you for......

_____
_____
_____
_____

Date _____

MY VERSE OF THE DAY

Be strong and be brave. Don't be afraid of those people because the Lord your God is with you. He will not fail you or leave you.
Deuteronomy 31:6 ERV

A person I am grateful for....

_____
_____
_____
_____
_____

One thing I liked about yesterday....

_____
_____
_____
_____
_____

I am grateful for....

One thing in nature, I am grateful God created.
(Draw it below)

Dear Jesus, thank you for......

_____
_____
_____
_____

Date _____

MY VERSE OF THE DAY

You will not have to do anything but stay calm.
The Lord will do the fighting for you.
Exodus 14:14 ERV

A person I am grateful for....

_____
_____
_____
_____
_____

One thing I liked about yesterday....

_____
_____
_____
_____
_____

I am grateful for....

One thing in nature, I am grateful God created.
(Draw it below)

Dear Jesus, thank you for......

_____
_____
_____
_____

You are God's amazing creation

Circle ALL the words that make your heart happy!

I'm thankful for....

Jesus	family	water
uncles	sleep	spring
animals	autumn	dad
grandparents'	doctors	school
roads'	clothes	food
ocean	air conditioning	fireplace
winter	nature	home
church	summer	aunts
friends	mum	pets
bed	park	nurses
car	teachers	bible

www.ingramcontent.com/pod-product-compliance
Lightning Source LLC
Chambersburg PA
CBHW082336300426
44109CB00046B/2505